Prince
h

The biography

Introduction

Prince Philip was born on the island of Corfu in Greece, on June 10, 1921. As members of Greek and Danish royalty, Philip and his family were banished from his native country when he was young, with the boy subsequently living in France, Germany and Britain.

Philip married Queen Elizabeth II before her ascension to the British throne in 1952. Their children include Prince Charles, heir apparent to the throne, Anne, Andrew and Edward. Philip served as the British royal consort for more than six decades.

Queen Elizabeth II became queen on February 6, 1952, and was crowned on June 2, 1953. She is the mother of Prince Charles, heir to the throne, as well as the grandmother of Princes William and Harry.

As the longest-serving monarch in British history, she has tried to make her reign more modern and sensitive to a changing public while maintaining traditions associated with the crown.

This is the descriptive, concise biography of Prince Philip & Queen Elizabeth II.

Table of Contents

Enjoy all our books for free...

  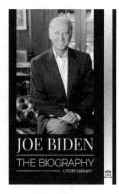

Interesting biographies, engaging introductions, and more.

Join the exclusive United Library reviewers club!

You will get a new book delivered in your inbox every Friday.

Join us today, go to: https://campsite.bio/unitedlibrary

Part 1: Prince Philip, Duke of Edinburgh

Prince Philip, Duke of Edinburgh, born Prince **Philip of Greece and Denmark** on June 10, 1921 in Corfu (Greece) and died on April 9, 2021 in Windsor (United Kingdom), is the husband of Elizabeth II, Queen of the United Kingdom and the other Commonwealth realms.

The fifth child and only son of Prince Andrew of Greece and Princess Alice of Battenberg, he is the grandson of King George I of Greece and a first cousin of Kings George II and Paul I. He is also a grandnephew of the last tsarina Alexandra Fyodorovna Romanova and of Princess Irene of Prussia, sister-in-law of the German emperor William II.

A member of the German-Danish house of Schleswig-Holstein-Sonderburg-Glücksburg, Prince Philip was born into the royal family of Greece, but his family went into exile as a child. After studying in Germany, England and Scotland, he joined the Royal Navy at the age of 18 in 1939. In July 1939, he began corresponding with Princess Elizabeth, the eldest daughter and heir apparent to King George VI. During World War II, he served in the Mediterranean and Pacific fleets. After the war, Philip obtained permission from George VI to marry Elizabeth. Before the engagement was officially announced, he renounced his Greek and Danish royal titles and predicates, converted from Greek Orthodox to Anglicanism and became a naturalized British subject, adopting the surname Mountbatten from his British maternal grandparents.

After five months of engagement, he became *Lieutenant* **Philip Mountbatten** and married Princess Elizabeth on November 20, 1947. On his wedding day, he received from his father-in-law the predicate of Royal Highness and the title of Duke of Edinburgh. Philip left active service, having attained the rank of *Commander*, when Elizabeth became Queen in 1952. His wife made him Prince of the United Kingdom in 1957 and Lord Grand Admiral in 2011. Philip has four children with Elizabeth: Charles, Anne, Andrew and Edward. Since an Order in Council in 1960, descendants of Philip and Elizabeth who do not hold royal titles can use the surname Mountbatten-Windsor. An avid sportsman, Philip helped develop the sport of horse driving. He is president of more than 800 organizations and chairman of the *Duke of Edinburgh's Award* for people aged 14 to 24.

Retired from public life as of 2017, he died two months shy of his 100th birthday. He is the longest-serving consort of the United Kingdom as well as the longest-serving spouse of a reigning British monarch (over 69 years).

Biography

Childhood

Prince Philip of Greece and Denmark was born on June 10, 1921 at the Palace of Mon Repos, on the island of Corfu in Greece. He is the only son and the fifth child of prince André of Greece and princess Alice of Battenberg, after his four elder sisters princesses Marguerite, Théodora, Cécile and Sophie. As a member of the House of Schleswig-Holstein-Sonderburg-Glücksburg, itself a branch of the House of Oldenburg, and as a male descendant of King George I of the Hellenes and King Christian IX of Denmark, he was both Prince of Greece and Prince of Denmark. At his birth, he is part of the order of succession to the throne of both kingdoms. However, in 1953, the *Law of Succession* abolished the rights of succession to the Danish throne for his family branch.

Shortly after Philip's birth, his maternal grandfather, Louis Mountbatten (born Louis de Battenberg), Marquis of Milford Haven, died. Louis was a British citizen by naturalization, who, after a career in the Royal Navy, had renounced his German titles and adopted the surname Mountbatten - an anglicized version of Battenberg - during World War I, due to anti-German sentiment in the United Kingdom. After traveling to London for the latter's memorial, Philip and his mother returned to Greece, where Prince Andrew had remained to command a division of the army involved in the Greco-Turkish War (1919-1922).

However, the war turned out badly for Greece and the Turks made important gains. On September 22, 1922, Philip's uncle, King Constantine I, was forced to abdicate and the new military government arrested Prince Andrew, along with others. The commander of the army, General Georgios Hatzianestis, and five high ranking politicians were executed. Prince Andre's life was then considered to be in danger, and Alice was placed under surveillance. In December, a revolutionary court banished Prince Andrew from Greece for life. The ship of the British navy HMS *Calypso* evacuates the family of prince André. Prince Philippe is put in safety in a camp bed made of a case of oranges. The family of Philip went to France, where they settled in rue du Mont-Valérien in Saint-Cloud, in the suburbs of Paris, in a house that had been lent to them by his rich aunt, the princess Marie Bonaparte.

Youth and education

He spent his childhood in France where his parents settled with Princess Marie Bonaparte and her husband, George of Greece. Philip began his education at an American school in Paris run by Donald MacJannet, who described Philip as a "robust, noisy...but always remarkably polite boy." Among his schoolmates was Anne of Bourbon-Parme, who later married Michael I. In 1928, he was sent to the United Kingdom to the *Cheam School*, living with his maternal grandmother and his uncle, George Mountbatten, at Kensington Palace or Lynden Manor in Bray, Berkshire. Over the next three years, his four sisters married German princes and moved to Germany, while his mother was placed in an asylum after being diagnosed as schizophrenic and his father moved to a small apartment in Monte Carlo. Philip had little contact with his mother for the rest of his childhood. In 1933, he was sent to the Schloss Salem School in Germany, which had the "advantage of saving school fees" because the school was owned by the family of his brother-in-law, Berthold of Baden. With the rise of Nazism in Germany, Salem's Jewish founder Kurt Hahn fled persecution and founded the Gordonstoun School in Scotland. After two terms at Salem, Philip moved to Gordonstoun. In 1937, his sister Cécile, her husband (Georges-Donatus, heir grand duke of Hesse), their two young sons and the grand duke's mother died in a plane crash in Ostend; Philip, who was only sixteen years old at the time, attended the funeral in Darmstadt. The following year, his uncle and guardian George Mountbatten, [2nd] Marquess of Milford Haven, died of bone cancer.

Military career

After leaving Gordonstoun in 1939, Prince Philip joined the Royal Navy, where he distinguished himself the following year at the Britannia Royal Naval College in Dartmouth as the top cadet in his class. He was commissioned as a midshipman in January 1940 and spent four months on the battleship HMS *Ramillies* protecting Australian Expeditionary Force convoys in the Indian Ocean, followed by shorter stints on the ships *Kent*, *Shropshire* and in Ceylon (now Sri Lanka).

After the Italian invasion of Greece in October 1940, he was transferred from the Indian Ocean to the battleship

HMS *Valiant* of the Mediterranean Fleet. Among other missions, he participated in the Battle of Crete, and was cited for his behavior during the Battle of Cape Matapan, where he was in charge of the battleship's searchlight control.

Philip received a citation in the order of the Royal Navy on February 3, 1942 as well as the French Croix de Guerre 1939-45 with palm. He also received the Greek War Cross of Valor. He held less prestigious positions such as head of the boiler room on the transport ship *RMS Empress of Russia*.

Philip was promoted to Sub-Lieutenant after a series of courses in Portsmouth where he finished first in four of the five classes. In June 1942, he was assigned to the former V and W class destroyer reclassified as an anti-aircraft escort, HMS *Wallace,* which was tasked with escorting convoys on the east coast of England, as well as for the Allied invasion of Sicily. He was promoted to the rank of lieutenant on July 16, 1942. In October of the same year, at the age of 21, he was appointed First Lieutenant of the destroyer HMS *Wallace,* making him one of the youngest First Officers in the Royal Navy. During the invasion of Sicily in July 1943, while still First Officer of HMS *Wallace*, he managed to launch a raft with smoke which distracted the bombers enough to allow the ship to escape unnoticed. In 1944, he was again assigned to a newer destroyer, the W-class HMS *Whelp, which was* part of the British Pacific Fleet in the 27th Destroyer Flotilla. He was present in Tokyo Bay for the signing of the Japanese surrender documents. In January 1946, Philip returned to the United Kingdom on HMS *Whelp* and was assigned as an instructor at the Petty Officers' School, the *Stone frigate* HMS *Royal Arthur*, based in Corsham, Wiltshire.

He was promoted to Lieutenant Commander in 1950, then *Commander* in 1952 and finally Admiral in 1953.

He is Honorary Colonel-in-Chief of six Canadian units: the Cameron Highlanders of Ottawa, the Queen's Own Cameron Highlanders of Canada, The Royal Canadian Army Cadets, the Royal Canadian Regiment, the Royal Hamilton Light Infantry (Wentworth Regiment) and the Seaforth Highlanders of Canada. He is Honorary President of the Naval Officers Association of Canada and the Royal Canadian Regiment Association, and Honorary Commodore of the Royal Canadian Naval Sailing Association.

On his 90th birthday in 2011, he was appointed Lord Grand Admiral of the Royal Navy, Honorary Admiral of Maritime Command (now the Royal Canadian Navy), General of Land Force Command (now the Canadian Army) and Air Command (now the Royal Canadian Air Force).

Wedding

In 1939, King George VI and Queen Elizabeth visited the Britannia Royal Naval College in Dartmouth. During this visit, the Queen and Lord Mountbatten asked Philip to accompany the royal couple's two daughters, Elizabeth and Margaret, his eighth cousins by Queen Victoria, and seventh by King Christian IX. Finally, in the summer of 1946, Philip asked the king for his daughter's hand in marriage. The King accepted his request, but would not give any formal commitment until Elizabeth's twenty-first birthday the following April. In the meantime, Philip renounced his Greek and Danish royal titles and his allegiance to the Greek crown, converted from Greek Orthodoxy to Anglicanism and became a British subject by naturalization, all of which was completed on March 18, 1947. Philip Mountbatten took his mother's surname. The engagement was announced to the public on July 10, 1947. The day before his wedding, King George VI awarded Philip the predicate of Royal Highness and on the morning of the wedding, November 20, 1947, he was made Duke of Edinburgh, Earl of Merioneth and Baron of Greenwich.

Philip and Elizabeth were married in Westminster Abbey. The ceremony was recorded and broadcast by the BBC to 200 million people around the world. However, in post-war England, it was not acceptable for the Duke of Edinburgh's German relations to be invited to the wedding, including his three surviving sisters, all of whom had married German princes, some with Nazi connections. After their marriage, the Duke and Duchess of Edinburgh took up residence at Clarence House. Their first two children were born there: Prince Charles in 1948 and Princess Anne in 1950.

Philip was keen to continue his career in the navy, well aware that his wife's future role as queen would eventually overshadow his ambitions. Nevertheless, Philip returned to the navy after his honeymoon, first in a clerical job at the Admiralty and later as head of the *Old Royal Naval College* in Greenwich. In 1949 he was stationed in Malta, having been appointed First Lieutenant of the destroyer *HMS Chequers*, the flagship of the 1st Destroyer Flotilla of the Mediterranean Fleet. In July 1950, he was promoted to Lieutenant Commander and commanded the frigate *HMS Magpie*. He was appointed Commanding Officer in 1952 of HMS *Chequers,* but his active naval career had ended in July 1951.

Prince Consort

Accession to the title

On his wife's accession to the throne on February 6, 1952, he became Prince of the United Kingdom and no longer had a surname. From then on, he was considered Prince Consort, although he never received the title. He gave up his military career to become a personal adviser to the Queen. In 1953, he was appointed Admiral of the Royal Navy, Marshal of the Royal Air Force and British Marshal. He was made *Prince of the United Kingdom of Great Britain and Northern Ireland* by his wife on February 22, 1957. The couple has four children:

- Charles, Prince of Wales, born November 14, 1948;
- Anne, royal princess, born on August 15, 1950;
- Andrew, Duke of York, born February 19, 1960;
- Edward, Earl of Wessex, born March 10, 1964.

Philip Mountbatten is an eight-time grandfather (of William, Harry, Peter, Zara, Beatrice, Eugenie, Louise and James), and a ten-time great-grandfather (of George, Charlotte, Louis, Archie, Savannah, Isla, Mia, Lena, Lucas and August).

Mountbatten or Windsor

Princess Elizabeth's accession to the throne raised the question of the name of the royal house. Prince Philip's uncle, Louis Mountbatten, argued for the name "House of Mountbatten", since Elizabeth had effectively assumed the latter name of Philip at their marriage. However, Queen Mary was hostile to this proposal because of the morganatic character of the House of Battenberg from which the Mountbattens came. It was on her advice that Prime Minister Winston Churchill interceded with the Queen to keep the royal house as the House of Windsor. The Duke of Edinburgh lamented that he was the only man in the country who could not pass on his name to his children.

It was not until 1960, after the death of Queen Mary and the resignation of Churchill, that an order-in-council specified that all male descendants of Philip, and therefore Elizabeth II, who did not bear the predicate of Royal Highness would take the name Mountbatten-Windsor (two of her grandchildren, Peter and Zara Phillips, bear their father's surname, as the British Royal Family is their maternal family). After her accession to the throne, the Queen made it clear that on all occasions, except in Parliament, the Duke of Edinburgh took precedence over other members of the Royal Family, including her son the Prince of Wales.

Activities

A great lover of polo, he founded the *Household Brigade Polo Club* on January 25, 1955, which became the *Guards Polo Club* in 1969. From 1964 to 1986, he was President of the International Equestrian Federation. Between 1960 and 1977, Prince Philip was President of the Zoological Society of London, which honored him as an honorary member in 1977.

He was the founder and first president of WWF-UK from 1961 to 1982, and then president of the World Wildlife Fund (WWF) International from 1981 to 1996. In this position, he founded the Alliance of Religions and Conservation in 1995.

Official duties

As Prince Consort, Philip assists his wife in her duties as sovereign by accompanying her to many dinners and ceremonies such as the opening of Parliament.

In 1981, Prince Philip interceded with his son Charles to get engaged or break up with Lady Diana Spencer. Faced with the injunctions of his father, Charles published the banns and married Diana six months later. In 1992, Charles and Diana's marital problems forced the Queen and the Duke of Edinburgh to try to reconcile them, without success. Philip writes his astonishment to Diana about Charles' extramarital affair with Camilla Parker Bowles. The couple divorced despite the efforts of the royal couple.

Suffering from a bladder infection, he was hospitalized, on June 4, 2012, during the festivities of the diamond jubilee of Elizabeth II, and then on August 16, 2012, following a relapse.

On May 4, 2017, Buckingham Palace announced in a press release that "His Royal Highness The Duke of Edinburgh has decided not to honor any more public engagements from the fall" and to retire from public life. He made his last public engagement on August 2, 2017. He has since made only three exceptions by attending the weddings of three of his grandchildren (the wedding of Prince Harry and Meghan Markle on May 19, 2018, the wedding of Princess Eugenie and Jack Brooksbank on October 12, 2018, and the wedding of Princess Beatrice and Edoardo Mapelli Mozzi on July 17, 2020).

Retirement

On April 3, 2018, Principle Philip was admitted to the King Edward VII Hospital for hip surgery, which took place the next day. He left the hospital the following April 13.

He was involved in a car accident on Jan. 17, 2019, while parking on a road near the Sandringham estate, where he lives in seclusion. An official statement says he is not injured. The driver and a passenger in the other car are taken to hospital. Philip went to the hospital the next morning as a precautionary measure. After apologizing, he voluntarily surrendered his driver's license three weeks later. On February 14, the Crown Prosecution Service announced that prosecuting Philip would not be "in the public interest. The Duke is still allowed to drive on private estates, however, and has been spotted driving in the grounds of Windsor Castle in April 2019.

From December 20 to 24, 2019, Philip is again staying at the King Edward VII Hospital, where he is being treated for a "pre-existing condition," in a visit described by Buckingham Palace as a "precautionary measure." The Duke had not been seen in public since attending Lady Gabriella Kingston's wedding in May 2019. A photo of Philip with the queen, while they are isolated at Windsor Castle due to the Covid-19 pandemic, is released on his 99th birthday in June 2020.

On February 16, 2021, he was again hospitalized "as a precaution" at the King Edward VII Hospital in London. The royal family said in a statement that the prince "was admitted to hospital after feeling indisposed and must remain for a few days for observation," before announcing that the Duke of Edinburgh was being treated for an infection. On March [1,] 2021, he was transferred to St. Bartholomew's Hospital, another London hospital, to undergo heart tests. On March 3, Prince Philip underwent heart surgery. He was transferred back to King Edward VII Hospital two days later. The Duke of Edinburgh finally left the hospital on March 16, 2021.

Death and tributes

Philip Mountbatten died on April 9, 2021 at Windsor Castle, at 99 years and 10 months. The royal family said that the prince died "peacefully". His death caused great emotion in the United Kingdom and around the world; many political figures paid tribute to him and flags were flown at half-mast. British Prime Minister Boris Johnson said that "the nation and the kingdom offer their thanks for the extraordinary life and work of Prince Philip, Duke of Edinburgh. In Scotland, Nicola Sturgeon said she was "saddened" and emphasized the "deep and enduring bond" she had with Prince Philip. Arlene Foster, First Minister of Northern Ireland, recalled that "the Prince was widely respected for his active and dedicated service to his country and for his unwavering support for Her Majesty the Queen during her reign. David Cameron said that Prince Philip is a "man who has dedicated his life to his country", and that "it has been an honor and a privilege to serve alongside the Duke of Edinburgh", who "has left an incredible legacy, and supported many associations and institutions with noble causes".

The Belgian Royal Family tweeted: "It is with great sadness that we learned of the death of His Royal Highness Prince Philip, Duke of Edinburgh. We extend our deepest condolences to Her Majesty The Queen and the British Royal Family and the people of the United Kingdom. Justin Trudeau, Prime Minister of Canada, salutes "a man of conviction and principle, driven by his sense of duty to others. Indian Prime Minister Narendra Modi paid tribute to the Prince's military career: "My thoughts are with the British people and the Royal Family. He had a remarkable career in the military and was at the forefront of many social initiatives. May he rest in peace. Israeli Prime Minister Benjamin Netanyahu expressed his "deepest condolences to Her Majesty Queen Elizabeth, Prince Charles, the Royal Family and the British people on the death of the Duke of Edinburgh. Prince Philip will be greatly missed in Israel and around the world. The President of the French Republic Emmanuel Macron expresses his "sincere condolences to Her Majesty Queen Elizabeth, the Royal Family and the British people on the death of His Royal Highness Prince Philip, who lived an exemplary life tinged with bravery, a sense of duty and a commitment to youth and the environment.

Philip Mountbatten's death led to the beginning of Operation *Forth Bridge*, a period of national mourning for eight days before the organization of his funeral, which was not national in accordance with the wishes of the Duke of Edinburgh but military, and which was held in St. George's Chapel at Windsor Castle.

Worship

For a few hundred villagers on the southwestern island of Tanna, Vanuatu, who practice a local derivation of the John Frum cult, Prince Philip is a deity related to the spirits of the Yasur volcano.

In popular culture

Cinema

In Stephen Frears' film, *The Queen*, released in 2006, the prince is played by the American actor James Cromwell.

He is one of the characters in the animated film *Royal Corgi* (2019).

Television

In the TV series *The Crown*, which has been on Netflix since 2016, his role is played by Matt Smith during the first two seasons, as well as by Finn Elliot for the scenes marking the prince's childhood. The role is then taken over by Tobias Menzies during the third and fourth season. It is the actor Jonathan Pryce who will take over the role of the husband of Queen Elizabeth, played by Imelda Staunton, for the fifth and sixth seasons of the series.

The program *Secrets d'Histoire* on France 3 of February 10, 2020, entitled *Prince Philip in the service of His Majesty*, is devoted to him.

Titles and honors

Full title

Philip has held many titles. Born Prince of Greece and Denmark, he renounced his royal titles and predicates just before his marriage to Princess Elizabeth and was created Duke of Edinburgh. He was granted the title of Prince of the United Kingdom in 1957 by letters patent from his wife. He is addressed as "my lord" (in English, *Sir*).

His titles were successively :

- *His Royal Highness* Prince Philip of Greece and Denmark (1921-1947) ;
- *Sir* Philip Mountbatten (1947);
- *His Royal Highness* the Duke of Edinburgh (1947-1957);
- *His Royal Highness* Prince Philip, Duke of Edinburgh (1957-2021).

His full title is: *His Royal Highness* Prince Philip, Duke of Edinburgh, Earl of Merioneth and Baron Greenwich, KG (Knight of the Garter), KT (Knight of the Thistle), OM (Order of Merit), GBE (Knight Grand Cross of the Order of the British Empire), AK (Knight of the Order of Australia), QSO (Companion of the Order of the Queen's Service), PC (Queen's Privy Council)

Part 2: Queen Elizabeth II of Great Britain

Elizabeth II (born April 21, 1926 in London) is Queen of the United Kingdom of Great Britain and Northern Ireland and fifteen other sovereign states, known as the Commonwealth realms, and their territories and dependencies. She is also the head of the Commonwealth, an organization of fifty-three states.

When her father George VI acceded to the throne in 1936 following the abdication of his brother Edward VIII, she became, at the age of 10, the heir apparent to the British Crown. During the Second World War, she enlisted in the Auxiliary Territorial Service. On November 20, 1947, she married Philip Mountbatten, Prince of Greece and Denmark, with whom she had four children: Charles, Prince of Wales, Anne, Princess Royal, Andrew, Duke of York and Edward, Earl of Wessex.

She acceded to the British throne on February 6, 1952 at the age of 25. Her coronation, on June 2, 1953, was the first to be broadcast on television. She became the sovereign of seven independent Commonwealth states: Australia, Canada, Ceylon, New Zealand, Pakistan, South Africa and the United Kingdom. Between 1956 and 1992, the number of its kingdoms changed as territories gained independence and some kingdoms became republics. In addition to Australia, Canada, New Zealand and the United Kingdom mentioned above, Elizabeth II is now Queen of Jamaica, the Bahamas, Grenada, Papua New Guinea, the Solomon Islands, Tuvalu, St. Lucia, St. Vincent and the Grenadines, Belize, Antigua and Barbuda, St. Kitts and Nevis and, until November 2021, Barbados.

During a long reign in which she saw fifteen British Prime Ministers pass through, she made many historic visits and oversaw several constitutional changes in her realms, such as the devolution of power to the United Kingdom and the repatriation of the Canadian Constitution. She also faced difficult times, such as the assassination of Prince Philip's uncle, Louis Mountbatten, the separations and divorce of three of her children in 1992 (a year she called *annus horribilis*), the death of her daughter-in-law, Diana Spencer, in 1997, and the deaths of her mother and sister in 2002. The Queen has faced strong criticism of the Royal Family from the press, but support for the monarchy and her personal popularity remain high among the British people.

Since September 9, 2015, she has been the longest reigning British sovereign (to date 69 years, 2 months and 4 days), surpassing the reign of her great-great-grandmother Queen Victoria (63 years, 7 months and 2 days). On October 13, 2016, following the death of Thailand's King Rama IX, she became the longest reigning and oldest sovereign currently in office.

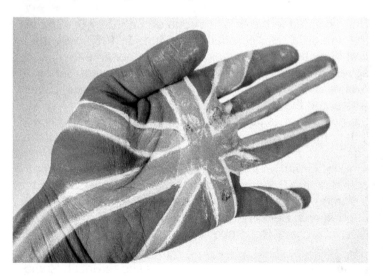

Early years

Birth and family

Elizabeth Alexandra Mary was the first child of Prince Albert, Duke of York (later George VI) and his wife, Elizabeth Bowes-Lyon. Her father was the second son of King George V and Queen Mary and her mother was the youngest daughter of the Scottish aristocrat Claude Bowes-Lyon, Lord Strathmore. Elizabeth was born by Caesarean section at 2:40 a.m. on April 21, 1926 at her maternal grandparents' London home at 17 Bruton Street in Mayfair. She was baptized by the Archbishop of York, Cosmo Lang, in the private chapel at Buckingham Palace on May 29. She was named Elizabeth after her mother, Alexandra after her great-grandmother the Queen Mother of King George V, who had died six months earlier, and Mary after her paternal grandmother, Queen Mary. Her relatives called her "Lilibet". George V adored his granddaughter, and when he became seriously ill in 1929, the popular press and his later biographers attributed his recovery to frequent visits from the three-year-old Elizabeth. As the great-great-granddaughter of Queen Victoria, Empress of India who died in 1901, she knew the three youngest children of her famous great-great-grandmother and can be considered a Victorian child.

Childhood

Queen Elizabeth had a sister, Margaret, four years her junior. The two princesses were educated at home under the supervision of their mother and governess, Marion Crawford, nicknamed "Crawfie. Education focused on history, elocution, literature and music. To the dismay of the royal family, Crawford published a book in 1950 about Elizabeth and Margaret's childhood, *The Little Princesses*, in which she described Elizabeth's love of horses and dogs, her discipline and sense of responsibility. Others corroborate these observations; Winston Churchill wrote of Elizabeth when she was two years old: "She has a commanding air and a reflexivity that is astonishing for a child. Her cousin Margaret Rhodes described her as "a jovial but extremely sensible and well-behaved little girl. In 1933, at the age of seven, the princess was portrayed by the royal court and aristocratic painter Philip de Laszlo.

Heir apparent

Abdication crisis of Edward VIII

As the granddaughter of a monarch in the male line, the granddaughter's full predicate and title is *Her Royal Highness Princess Elizabeth of York*. She was then third in line to the British throne after her uncle, Edward of Wales, and her father, the Duke of York. Although her birth attracted public attention, she was not expected to ever become queen, as the Prince of Wales was only 31 years old and many believed he would marry and have children. In 1936, when her grandfather King George V died, her uncle ascended the throne as Edward VIII and she became the second in line of succession. In December 1936, Edward VIII abdicated (his intention to marry Wallis Simpson, twice divorced, caused a constitutional crisis). Elizabeth's father became king as George VI and she became, at the age of 10, the heir apparent with the title of *Her Royal Highness Princess Elizabeth*. If her parents had had a son later, she would have lost her position as heir apparent and her brother would have become the crown prince to the British throne. Elizabeth received private instruction in constitutional history from Henry Marten, the vice president of Eton College, and learned French from native French-speaking governesses. A guiding company, the first company at Buckingham Palace, was specially formed so that she could meet girls her own age.

In 1939, Elizabeth's parents travelled to Canada and the United States. As in 1927, when they went to Australia and New Zealand, Elisabeth stayed in the United Kingdom, as her father considered her too young for such trips. Elisabeth "seemed on the verge of tears" when her parents left. They exchanged letters regularly and, on May 18, made the first transatlantic phone call of the royal family.

World War II

On September 3, 1939, the United Kingdom entered the Second World War. During this period of conflict, while English cities were frequently bombed by the German air force, children were evacuated to rural areas. Politician Douglas Hogg suggested that the two princesses be evacuated to Canada, but this proposal was refused by Elizabeth's mother, who declared: "My children will not go anywhere without me. I will not go without the King. And the king will never leave. "Princesses Elizabeth and Margaret remained at Balmoral Castle in Scotland until Christmas 1939, when they were moved to Sandringham House in Norfolk. From February to May 1940, they resided at Royal Lodge in Windsor's Great Park before moving to Windsor Castle, where they remained for most of the war. At Windsor, Elizabeth held a pantomime at Christmas to support the Queen's Wool Fund, which purchased wool for knitting military clothing. In 1940, at the age of 14, she gave her first radio address to evacuated children during a BBC children's program:

"We try to do all we can to help our brave sailors, soldiers and airmen and we also try to bear our share of the danger and sadness of war. We know, each of us, that it will all end well. »

In 1943, at the age of 16, Elizabeth made her first public appearance alone at an inspection of the Grenadier Guards, of which she had been appointed Colonel-in-Chief the previous year. As she approached her 18th birthday, the law was changed so that she could become one of the five State Councillors (en) in case of her father's incapacity or during a trip abroad, as during her visit to Italy in July 1944. In February 1945, she joined the Auxiliary Territorial Service with the honorary rank of second *subaltern*. She received training in driving and mechanics, and was promoted to *junior commander* five months later.

On May 8, 1945, the day Nazi Germany surrendered, Princess Elizabeth and Princess Margaret mingled anonymously with the jubilant crowd in the streets of London. In one of her few interviews, Elizabeth said: "We asked our parents if we could go out and see for ourselves. I remember we were terrified that we would be recognized... I remember the lines of strangers holding hands and walking down Whitehall, all together in a tide of happiness and relief. »

During the war, the government sought on several occasions to appease Welsh nationalism by bringing Elizabeth closer to Wales. It was suggested that the princess become constable of Caernarfon Castle, a position then held by David Lloyd George. The Secretary of State for the Interior, Herbert Morrison, considered appointing her as head of the Urdd Gobaith Cymru (en), the Welsh youth organization. Welsh politicians proposed that Elizabeth become Princess of Wales on her 18th birthday. However, these plans were abandoned for various reasons, including the fear that Elizabeth would be associated with conscientious objectors in the Urdd. In 1946, she joined the Gorsedd of the Bards of the Isle of Britain at the Eisteddfod Genedlaethol.

In 1947, Princess Elisabeth made her first trip abroad by accompanying her parents to southern Africa. During this trip, on her 21st birthday, she made a radio address to the Commonwealth, in which she promised to

"I declare before you all that I will devote my whole life, whether long or short, to your service and to the service of the great imperial family of which we are all a part. »

Wedding

Elisabeth met her future husband, Prince Philip of Greece and Denmark (five years her senior), in 1934, and saw him again in 1937. They are first cousins by the King of Denmark, Christian IX, and second cousins by Queen Victoria. They met again at the *Royal Naval College* in Dartmouth in July 1939. When she was only 13 years old, Elizabeth declared that she had fallen in love with Philip, and they began to exchange letters. Their engagement was officially announced on July 9, 1947.

This relation is not then without controversy, Philip being only a member of a younger branch of the Royal House of Greece, and the Greek monarchy having known many vicissitudes since the beginning of the century. Moreover, this prince of foreign origin (even if he was naturalized following his service in the *Royal Navy* during the Second World War) was not particularly rich. Some of his sisters married German princes close to the Nazi party. Marion Crawford writes: "Some of the king's advisers considered him not good enough for her. He was a prince without a house or kingdom. Some documents clearly and strongly supported Philip's foreign background. Later biographies suggest that Elizabeth's mother was initially opposed to the union, even calling Philip a Hun. At the end of her life, however, she told her biographer Tim Heald that Philip was an "English gentleman.

Before the wedding, Philip renounced his Greek and Danish titles, abandoned the Greek Orthodox Church for Anglicanism and adopted the title of *Lieutenant Philip Mountbatten*, taking his mother's British name. Just before the wedding, he was made Duke of Edinburgh and received the predicate of Royal Highness.

Elizabeth and Philip were married on November 20, 1947 at Westminster Abbey. They received about 2,500 gifts from all over the world. As the United Kingdom had not yet fully recovered from the war, Elizabeth imposed that ration coupons be used to buy the fabric for her dress, designed by Norman Hartnell. Philip's German relatives (including his three surviving sisters), as well as the Duke of Windsor (former King Edward VIII), were not invited to the ceremony.

Elizabeth gave birth to her first child, Charles, on November 14, 1948. A month earlier, the king issued letters patent authorizing his daughter's children to bear the title of prince or princess, which was theoretically prohibited because their father was no longer a royal prince. A second child, Princess Anne, was born on 15 August 1950.

Following his marriage, the couple rented *Windlesham Moor*, near Windsor Castle, until July 4, 1949, when they moved to *Clarence House* in London. On several occasions between 1949 and 1951, the Duke of Edinburgh was stationed in the British protectorate of Malta as an officer in the *Royal Navy*. He and Elizabeth then resided in the Maltese village of Gwardamanġa, where they rented the residence of Philip's uncle, Louis Mountbatten. During this period, their children remain in the United Kingdom.

Queen of the United Kingdom and other Commonwealth Realms

Accession to the throne and coronation

In 1951, George VI's health declined and Elizabeth frequently replaced him for public ceremonies. During her visit to North America, where she went to Canada and met President Truman in Washington in October 1951, her private secretary, Martin Charteris, carried with him a draft of a declaration of accession to the throne should the king die during his trip. In early 1952, Elizabeth and Philip undertook a tour of Australia and New Zealand with a stopover in Kenya. On February 6, 1952, they had just returned to their Kenyan home at *Sagana Lodge* from a visit to Aberdare National Park when they learned of the King's death. Martin Charteris asked her to choose a reigning name and she decided to keep Elizabeth, "of course". She was then proclaimed Queen in all her kingdoms as Elizabeth II (an Elizabeth who had previously reigned in the 16th century) and the court members hastily returned to the UK. As the new monarch, she took up residence at Buckingham Palace.

With Elizabeth's accession to the throne, it seemed likely that the Royal House would be named after her husband and become the *House of Mountbatten,* as was the custom for a woman to take her husband's name. Elizabeth's grandmother, Mary de Teck, and the Prime Minister of the United Kingdom, Winston Churchill, preferred to keep the name *House of Windsor* and the word *Windsor* was retained. The Duke complained that he "was the only man in the country who was not allowed to name his own children after himself. In 1960, after Mary de Teck's death in 1953 and Churchill's resignation in 1955, the name *Mountbatten-Windsor* was adopted for Philip and his male descendants who did not bear royal titles.

In the midst of preparations for the coronation, Princess Margaret informed her sister that she wished to marry the aviator Peter Townsend, 16 years her senior and with two children from a previous marriage. The Queen asked her to wait a year; according to Martin Charteris, "the Queen was naturally sympathetic to the Princess, but I think she imagined, hoped, that in time the affair would wear off on its own. Political leaders were opposed to the union and the Church of England did not allow remarriage unless the divorced man was widowed. If Margaret performed a civil marriage, it was likely that she would have to renounce her right to the throne. She finally decided to abandon her relationship with Townsend. In 1960 she married Antony Armstrong-Jones who was made Earl of Snowdon the following year. They divorced in 1978 and she did not remarry.

Despite Queen Mary's death on March 24, preparations for the coronation continued and it took place as planned on June 2, 1953. With the exception of the Eucharist and the anointing, the entire ceremony at Westminster Abbey was televised for the first time in history. The coronation robe was designed by Norman Hartnell and was embroidered with the floral emblems of the Commonwealth countries: the English Tudor rose, the Scottish thistle, the Welsh leek, the Irish shamrock, the Canadian maple leaf, the Australian golden mimosa, the New Zealand silver fern, the South African royal protée, the Indian and Ceylon lotus flower, and the Pakistani wheat, cotton and jute.

Post-war period (1952-1972)

The first two decades of the Queen's reign were just after the Second World War during the 1950s and 1960s. The period is marked by the Cold War politically and by the Trente Glorieuses economically.

Evolution of the Commonwealth

During her reign, Queen Elizabeth II witnessed the transformation of the British Empire into the Commonwealth. By the time of her accession to the throne in 1952, her role as head of state of multiple independent states had been established. Between 1953 and 1954, the Queen and her husband embarked on a six-month world tour. She became the first monarch of Australia and New Zealand to visit those countries. The Queen's visits drew large crowds and it is estimated that three quarters of the Australian population saw her on these occasions. During her reign, the Queen made more than 170 visits to Commonwealth states and nearly 100 to non-Commonwealth states, making her the most traveled head of state in history.

In 1956, French Prime Minister Guy Mollet and British Prime Minister Anthony Eden discussed the possibility of France joining the Commonwealth. The proposal was never accepted, and the following year France signed the Treaty of Rome establishing the European Economic Community, the precursor of the European Union. In November 1956, the United Kingdom and France invaded Egypt to regain control of the Suez Canal; the operation ended miserably and Eden resigned two months later. Louis Mountbatten claimed that the Queen was opposed to the offensive, but Eden denied this.

In 1957, she visited the United States and addressed the United Nations General Assembly on behalf of the Commonwealth. During the same diplomatic visit, she opened Canada's 23rd Parliament, becoming the first

Canadian monarch to open a session of Parliament. Two years later, solely in her capacity as Queen of Canada, she returned to the United States and visited Canada, having learned upon her arrival in St. John's, Newfoundland, that she was expecting her third child. In 1961 she visited Cyprus, India, Pakistan, Nepal and Iran. During a visit to Ghana that same year, she dismissed fears for her safety even though her host, President Kwame Nkrumah, who had replaced her as Ghana's head of state the previous year, was the target of assassins. Prior to her visit to Quebec in 1964, the press reported that extremists in the province's separatist movement were planning to assassinate her. There was no assassination attempt, but demonstrations broke out while she was in Quebec City; the queen's "calm and courage in the face of violence" was noted.

In addition to participating in traditional ceremonies, Elizabeth II introduced new practices such as the first royal walkabout, which took place during a tour of Australia and New Zealand in 1970.

The 1960s and 1970s saw an acceleration of decolonization in Africa and the Caribbean. More than twenty countries gained independence through negotiated transitions to greater autonomy. In 1965, however, the Prime Minister of Rhodesia unilaterally declared the country's independence from the United Kingdom in order to maintain white rule while expressing his "loyalty and devotion" to Elizabeth II. Although the Queen rejected it in a formal declaration and Rhodesia was hit by international sanctions, the Smith regime survived until 1979.

Influence on the Conservative Party

In the absence of a formal mechanism within the Conservative party to choose a new leader after Eden's resignation, it fell to the Queen to decide who should form a new government. Eden recommended that she consult Lord Salisbury, the Lord President of the Council. Lord Salisbury and Lord Kilmuir, the Lord Chancellor, sought the advice of the Cabinet and Winston Churchill and the Queen appointed the proposed candidate, Harold Macmillan.

The Suez crisis and the choice of Eden's successor led to the Queen's first major personal criticism in 1957. In a newspaper he owned and edited, Lord Altrincham accused her of being "out of her depth" and "unable to get more than a few sentences together without help. Altrincham's comments were condemned and he was physically assaulted. Six years later, in 1963, Macmillan resigned and advised the Queen to choose Alec Douglas-Home as her successor, which she did. She was again criticized for appointing a prime minister on the advice of a few or one minister. In 1965, the Conservatives adopted a new method of appointing their leader that no longer required the Queen to choose.

Royal family

During this period, she enlarged the royal family by having two more children in 1960 (Andrew) and 1964 (Edward). The pregnancies that preceded these births were the only occasions when she did not participate in the opening ceremony of the British Parliament during her reign.

She gave her eldest son Charles the title of Prince of Wales and Earl of Chester on 26 July 1958. However, his enthronement was not effective until July [1] 1969, when she gave him the crown of the princes of Wales at Caernarfon Castle, during a ceremony broadcast on British television. The prince pronounces a part of his speech in Welsh language.

The time of wars and crises (1973-1992)

The two decades of the 1970s and 1980s saw the kingdom join the EEC. This period was still marked by the Cold War politically, but unlike the previous two decades, the kingdom entered an economic recession after the two oil shocks of 1973 and 1979, followed by the economic liberalism of Margaret Thatcher and the Single European Act.

Entry into the EEC (1973)

On January 22, 1972, the British Prime Minister Edward Heath signed in Brussels the treaty of accession to the European Economic Community (EEC), confirmed by the European Communities Act 1972 voted by the House of Commons in third reading on July 13, 1972.

The Queen gave Royal Assent on October 17, 1972, allowing the United Kingdom to officially join the Community on January [1] 1973. The British people in turn confirmed membership by referendum on June 5, 1975.

Government crisis (1974)

In February 1974, British Prime Minister Edward Heath advised the Queen to call a general election while she was visiting the Pacific Islands, forcing her to return to the United Kingdom. The election resulted in a minority parliament and Heath resigned when negotiations to form a coalition government with the Liberal Party failed. The Queen took the initiative and asked the leader of the official opposition, Labour's Harold Wilson, to form a government.

Constitutional crisis in Australia (1975)

At the height of Australia's 1975 constitutional crisis, Australian Prime Minister Gough Whitlam was sacked by Governor-General John Kerr after the opposition-controlled Senate rejected Whitlam's budget proposals. With Gough Whitlam holding a majority in the House of Representatives, its Speaker Gordon Scholes appealed to the Queen to overturn Kerr's decision. Elizabeth II refused, saying she could not interfere in decisions that the Australian constitution reserved for the Governor-General. The crisis fuelled republican feelings in Australia.

Silver Jubilee (1977)

In 1977, Elizabeth II celebrated her Silver Jubilee, marking 25 years on the throne. Celebrations and ceremonies were held throughout the *Commonwealth* and were usually organized around the time of the Queen's visit. The festivities reaffirmed the Queen's popularity despite the negative media coverage of Princess Margaret's divorce.

Attacks (1981-1982)

In 1981, during the Salute to the Colors ceremony and six weeks before the wedding of Prince Charles and Diana Spencer, six shots were fired at the Queen as she rode down *The Mall* on her horse, Burmese. Police later discovered that the shots were blanks. The shooter, Marcus Sarjeant, was sentenced to five years in prison before being released after three years. The queen's composure and control of her mount was widely noted.

On July 9, 1982, the Queen was awakened in her room at Buckingham Palace by an intruder named Michael Fagan. Newspapers at the time reported that they talked for nearly ten minutes before security intervened, but Michael Fagan contradicted these claims.

Dissolution of constitutional ties with Canada (1982)

According to Canadian politician Paul Martin, in the late 1970s the Queen was concerned that the Crown "meant little" to Canadian Prime Minister Pierre Elliott Trudeau. British politician Tony Benn said the Queen found Trudeau "quite disappointing. Trudeau's supposed republicanism seemed to be confirmed by his antics such as slipping on the banisters at Buckingham Palace, pirouetting behind the Queen's back in 1977 and removing several Canadian royal symbols during his term.

In 1980, Canadian politicians went to London to discuss the repatriation of Canada's constitution and found the Queen "better informed...than any British politician or bureaucrat. She took a particular interest in the subject after the defeat of Canada's Bill C-60, which would have affected her status as head of state. The repatriation of 1982 removed the need to consult the British Parliament to amend the Canadian constitution, but the monarchy was retained. Trudeau stated in his memoirs that the Queen was supportive of his attempts at constitutional reform and that he was impressed by "the grace she had in public" and "the wisdom she showed in private.

In 1987 in Canada, the Queen publicly expressed her support for the Meech Lake Accord, a constitutional reform project that aimed to bring Quebec under the Constitution Act of 1982. The Queen's support divided the Canadian political class and she was criticized by opponents of these constitutional amendments, including Pierre Trudeau. Finally the project was rejected in 1990.

Falklands War (1982)

The Falklands War is a conflict between Argentina and the United Kingdom in the Falkland Islands and South Georgia and the South Sandwich Islands. It began on April 2, 1982 with the landing of the Argentine army and ended on June 14, 1982 with a cease-fire. It ended with a British victory that allowed the United Kingdom to assert its sovereignty over these territories.

The Queen was proud but also worried throughout this period about the fate of her second son Andrew who was fighting in the war as a helicopter pilot.

Invasion of Grenada (1983)

Elizabeth II welcomed US President Ronald Reagan to Windsor Castle in 1982 and visited his California ranch in 1983. This is why she was so irritated when the American administration launched the invasion of Grenada in 1983, one of her Caribbean kingdoms, without her prior knowledge.

Republic of Fiji (1987)

In 1987, Fiji's democratically elected government was overthrown in a coup. As monarch of Fiji, Elizabeth II supported the efforts of Governor General Penaia Ganilau to exercise executive power and find a way out of the crisis.

Nevertheless, the organizer of the coup, Sitiveni Rabuka, deposed Ganilau and abolished the monarchy.

Gulf War (1990-1991)

The Gulf War was a conflict between Iraq and a coalition of 35 states led by the United States from August 2, 1990 to February 28, 1991, following Iraq's invasion and annexation of Kuwait. After the coalition's victory, the Queen became the first British sovereign to address a joint session of the United States Congress.

Abolition of apartheid (1991)

Former Canadian Prime Minister Brian Mulroney said Elizabeth II played a "big role behind the scenes" in ending apartheid in South Africa in 1991.

The media and the Royal Family

The media's interest in the opinions and private lives of the royal family in the 1980s led to a series of sensational revelations, the veracity of which was not always established. As Kelvin MacKenzie, the editor of *The Sun,* told his staff, "Give me the royal family's antics. Don't worry if it's not true as long as there's not much trouble afterwards. The *Observer*'s editor, Donald Trelford, wrote in the September 21, 1986 issue: "The royal soap opera has reached such a level of public interest that the line between fiction and reality has been lost sight of... It is not just that some newspapers do not check their information or refuse to accept denials: they do not care whether the stories are true or not.

Relations with Margaret Thatcher

It was reported, mainly by the *Sunday Times*, that the Queen was concerned that British Prime Minister Margaret Thatcher's economic policies were deepening divisions in society and that she was alarmed by high unemployment, a series of riots in 1981, the violence of the miners' strike and the government's refusal to sanction the apartheid regime in South Africa. The rumours came from the Queen's assistant, Michael Shea, and the Secretary General of the Commonwealth, Shridath Ramphal, but Shea claimed that her words had been taken out of context and amplified by journalists. Thatcher was quoted as saying that the Queen would vote for her opponents in the Social Democratic Party. Thatcher's biographer, John Campbell, called it "an example of journalistic nonsense.

Contradicting reports of their poor relationship, Thatcher later expressed her personal admiration for the Queen and after she was replaced by John Major, the Queen made her a member of the Orders of Merit and the Garter.

The *annus horribilis* (1992)

In early 1991, press estimates of the queen's personal wealth that exceeded palace figures and revelations of adultery and strained marriages in the royal family weakened support for the monarchy in the United Kingdom. The queen's children's participation in a charity game show called *It's a Royal Knockout* was ridiculed in the press and the queen became a target of ridicule.

It was against this backdrop that the year 1992 began, which the Queen described as *annus horribilis* ("horrible year") in an address on November 24, 1992, marking 40 years on the throne. In March, her second son, Prince Andrew of York, and his wife Sarah Ferguson separated; in April, her daughter, Princess Anne, divorced her husband Mark Phillips; during an official visit to Germany in October, demonstrators in Dresden threw eggs at her; and in November, Windsor Castle was hit by a serious fire. The monarchy was criticized and this increased public dislike. In an unusually personal speech, the Queen said that any institution must expect criticism, but suggested that it should be made with "a touch of humour, delicacy and understanding. Two days later, Prime Minister John Major announced a reform of the monarchy's finances that resulted in a reduction of the civil list and forced the monarch to pay income tax for the first time in his history. In December, Prince Charles and his wife Diana Spencer officially announced their separation. The year ended with the Queen suing *The Sun* newspaper for copyright infringement for publishing the text of her Christmas address two days before it was broadcast. The newspaper was ordered to pay legal costs and £200,000 in compensation, which was donated to charity.

Reign in the European Union (1993-2020)

The kingdom accepts the liberal evolution of the EEC into the European Union during the three decades of the 1990s, 2000 and 2010.

Maastricht Treaty (1993)

The Treaty on European Union (or Maastricht Treaty) was signed on 7 February 1992 by British Prime Minister John Major. It is the founding treaty of the European Union.

The treaty was ratified by the House of Commons on May 20, 1993, and then by Royal Assent from the Queen. It came into force on November [1] 1993 without a referendum for the British people to ratify it.

Death of Diana (1997)

The revelations about Charles and Diana's marriage continued after their separation in 1992. Although republican ideas seemed to be more popular than ever in the United Kingdom, republicanism was still in the minority and the Queen retained high levels of approval. Critics focused more on the monarchical institution and the Queen's extended family than on her actions and behaviour. After discussions with Prime Minister John Major, Archbishop of Canterbury George Carey, her private secretary Robert Fellowes and her husband, she wrote to Charles and Diana at the end of December 1995 saying that a divorce was preferable.

A year after the divorce in 1996, Diana died in a car accident in Paris on August 31, 1997. The Queen was on vacation with Charles and her grandchildren, William and Harry, at Balmoral Castle. Diana's two children wanted to go to church and the royal couple accompanied them in the morning. After this one public appearance, the Queen and the Duke of Edinburgh protected their grandchildren from the media storm by keeping them at the castle for five days, but the public was dismayed that the royal family did not lower the flags at Buckingham Palace to half mast. Pressed by the backlash, the Queen returned to London and agreed to make a televised address on September 5, the day before Diana's funeral. She expressed her admiration for Diana and her "grandmotherly" feelings for Princes William and Harry; this act was appreciated by public opinion and hostility subsided.

Golden Jubilee (2002)

In 2002, Elizabeth II celebrated her Golden Jubilee of reign. With her sister and mother having died in February and March respectively, the media wondered whether the Jubilee would be a success or a failure. She again embarked on a long tour of her kingdoms, beginning in Jamaica in February, where she described her farewell banquet as "memorable" after a power failure left the Governor General's residence in darkness. As in 1977, joyous demonstrations took place at each of her trips and monuments were named in her honor. A million people attended the three days of Jubilee celebrations in London each day, and the enthusiasm shown by the crowds was far greater than journalists had anticipated.

Health problems

Although she had had few health problems during her life,
she had surgery on both knees in 2003. On October 9,
2004, she opened the Scottish Parliament building in
Edinburgh - although the members of the constituent
nation had held their first session there on September 7 -
as a result of the *Scotland Act 1998*.

In October 2006, she did not participate in the inauguration
of the new Emirates Stadium in London because of a
muscle tear in her back that had disabled her since the
summer.

Relations with Tony Blair

In May 2007, *The Daily Telegraph quoted* anonymous
sources as saying that the Queen was "exasperated and
disappointed" with Prime Minister Tony Blair's policies, that
she was concerned about troop fatigue in Iraq and
Afghanistan and that she had repeatedly expressed
concern about his rural policies. According to the same

sources, she nevertheless admired Blair's efforts to end the violence in Northern Ireland.

Reconciliation with Ireland

Ireland's relations with the Crown have been very tense since its independence on December 6, 1922 and since the proclamation of the republic on April 18, 1949. During her reign, the Queen was also deeply affected by the assassination of her uncle by marriage Louis Mountbatten, perpetrated by the Provisional Irish Republican Army on August 27, 1979.

On March 20, 2008, ten years after the Good Friday Agreement, the Queen attended the first Maundy Thursday Mass outside England and Wales, in the Church of Ireland's St. Patrick's Cathedral in Armagh (Northern Ireland).

At the invitation of the President of Ireland, Mary McAleese, the Queen made in May 2011, the first official visit of a British monarch to Ireland since its separation from the kingdom on December 6, 1922.

Last official trips (2010-2011)

Elizabeth II addressed the United Nations General Assembly for a second time as head of the *Commonwealth* in July 2010. During her visit to New York, which followed a visit to Canada, she opened a memorial garden for the British victims of the September 11, 2001 attacks. The Queen's visit to Australia in October 2011, her eleventh since 1954, was described by the press as a "farewell tour" because of her age.

Diamond Jubilee (2012)

The Diamond Jubilee of 2012 marks 60 years of Elizabeth II's reign and is once again being celebrated throughout the *Commonwealth*. In a statement issued on February 6, she said, "In this special year, as I rededicate myself to your service, I hope we will all remember the power of unity and the unifying force of family, friendship and neighbourliness... I also hope that this Jubilee year will be an opportunity to express our gratitude for the major advances made since 1952 and to look forward to the future with confidence." She and her husband toured the United Kingdom while her children and grandchildren represented her in the *Commonwealth* realms.

The Queen opens the Summer Olympics on July 27 and the Summer Paralympics on August 29, 2012 in London. She plays her own role in a short film as part of the opening ceremony with Daniel Craig in the role of James Bond. Her father had opened the 1948 Olympic Games in London, and her great-grandfather, Edward VII, those of 1908, also in London. Elizabeth II had also opened those of 1976 in Montreal and Philip those of 1956 in Melbourne. She is the first head of state to open two Olympics in two different countries.

In December 2012, she became the first British sovereign to attend a peacetime British cabinet meeting since George III in 1781, and Foreign Secretary William Hague announced shortly thereafter that the previously unnamed southern portion of the British Antarctic Territory would be named Queen Elizabeth Land in her honor.

Rehabilitation of Alan Turing (2013)

Alan Turing was a mathematician who committed suicide in 1954 because of his conviction for homosexuality. Turing had participated in the Second World War for MI6, deciphering German codes, but was sentenced shortly after to chemical castration.

Prime Minister Gordon Brown, on behalf of the British government, expressed his regrets in September 2009.

In December 2012, a group of eleven British scientists, including physicist Stephen Hawking, called on the British Government to overturn his conviction, posthumously.

Finally on December 24, 2013, Queen Elizabeth II signed a royal act of clemency, on the proposal of the Secretary of State for Justice Chris Grayling, who said that it was a conviction "that we would consider today to be unjust and discriminatory." This is the fourth time since 1945 that the royal prerogative of mercy has been exercised.

Scottish referendum (2014)

Even though the queen is bound by an unwavering reserve on the political affairs of her kingdom, the independence of Scotland does not leave her indifferent. She took advantage of her exit from mass on September 14, 2014, near her summer residence in Balmoral, to say a few words to the residents who had come to greet her: "I hope people will think carefully about the future before they go to vote on Thursday." This statement would be for many a sign that the queen wants the no to win four days later in the referendum on Scottish independence.Finally, it is the "no" that wins with 55.3% of votes cast.

Brexit (2016-2020)

After Prime Minister David Cameron held a referendum on June 23, 2016, on the United Kingdom's membership in the European Union, the British people voted in favor of withdrawal. The House of Commons authorized the government to begin the process of leaving the European Union on March 13, 2017, confirmed by royal assent from the queen three days later. Prime Minister Theresa May initiates the Article 50 process on March 29, 2017.

In her 2018 Christmas address, following tensions between her British subjects over the past three years, the Queen calls on them to show "respect" to each other, during this time of transition to Brexit. "Even if the deepest differences separate us, treating others with respect, as human beings, is always a good first step."

The Queen speaks of Brexit in a speech to the British Women's Institute on January 24, 2019: "In our search for new answers in these modern times, I for one prefer tried and true recipes, such as speaking to each other with respect and respecting different points of view, coming together to seek common ground, and never forgetting to stand back." In her 2019 Christmas address, she again calls on the British to overcome their divisions, "Small steps taken with faith and hope can overcome long-standing differences and deep divisions to bring harmony and understanding. »

The House of Commons votes definitively on January 9, 2020 on the withdrawal agreement signed on October 17, 2019, confirmed by Royal Assent on January 23, 2020. The United Kingdom officially leaves the European Union on January 31, 2020.

The post-European Union (since 2020)

Covid-19 pandemic

On March 19, 2020, Queen Elizabeth II retired as a precaution to Windsor Castle as the Covid-19 pandemic hit the United Kingdom. The 93-year-old sovereign had already announced in the previous days the postponement of several public engagements due to the pandemic. On April 5, 2020, Elizabeth II addressed the British nation and the Commonwealth in an exceptional televised address, the fourth since the beginning of her reign, recorded from Windsor Castle where the Queen is confined with her husband. She said: "I hope that in the years to come everyone can be proud of the way [the British people] have responded to this challenge. Those who come after us will say that the British of this generation were as strong as any. That the attributes of self-discipline, quiet resolve and comradeship still characterize this country. On May 8, the following year, on the occasion of the commemoration of the end of the Second World War, the Queen gave another speech, broadcast on the BBC at 8 p.m., the exact time her father King George VI had spoken on the radio in 1945, in which she called on the British people to "never lose hope.

The Queen resumes her official engagements in October 2020 on the occasion of an inauguration. She appeared for the first time in a mask on November 4, 2020, for the 100th anniversary of the burial of the Unknown Soldier at Westminster Abbey. The same month, because of the risk of contamination related to the virus, Elizabeth II and her husband Prince Philip return to Windsor Castle, about 40 km from London.

On January 9, 2021, Buckingham Palace announced that the Queen and her husband had received a first dose of Pfizer-BioNTech's Covid-19 vaccine. In February, the palace releases a video in which the Queen encourages Britons to get vaccinated, stressing that reluctant people "should think of others rather than themselves."

Death of Prince Philip (2021)

On April 9, 2021, after more than seventy-three years of marriage, her husband, Prince Philip, died at Windsor Castle at the age of 99. Queen Elizabeth II said in a statement that she was deeply affected by his death, saying that he was her strength. Philip was also considered the second "pillar" of the monarchy after her.

Future republic of Barbados

On September 16, 2020, the Governor General of Barbados, Sandra Mason, announced in a speech that her country would become a republic by November 30, 2021. In a speech given from the capital, she said, "Having achieved independence over half a century ago, our country can have no doubts about its capacity for self-government. The reign of Elizabeth II, who ascended the

Barbadian throne in 1966, is expected to end with the advent of the republic in Barbados.

Platinum Jubilee (2022)

In November 2020, Buckingham Palace announced that on the occasion of Elizabeth II's 70th year on the throne, the Queen's Platinum Jubilee would be celebrated over four public holidays in June 2022. Secretary of State for Culture Oliver Dowden says the celebrations, which will take place from June 2 to 4, will follow an extensive program of events, with state-of-the-art art and technology exhibitions. He says these will be interspersed with large "traditional bands from around the country and celebrations". The government also says that "spectacular moments in London and other major cities will be complemented by events in communities across the UK and the Commonwealth, allowing people to come together in celebration and thanksgiving at national and local levels" [source not available].

Longevity of the kingdom

Queen Elizabeth II is the oldest British monarch with the longest reign ahead of Victoria (since September 9, 2015). She has reigned for 69 years, and is the longest reigning monarch currently still in office since the death of Thailand's King Rama IX on October 13, 2016.

In November 2019, rumors relayed by some British media suggest that the queen would consider abdicating within "a few years," specifically on her 95th birthday in 2021, but people close to the royal family deny the rumors. The queen has no intention of abdicating, even though her public engagements are increasingly handled by her eldest son as the years go by.

The Queen celebrated her 94th birthday on April 21, 2020 during Covid-19, without the traditional 41 cannon shots fired from Hyde Park. In October 2020, while the Prince of Wales seems to be "preparing for his future role", in particular by separating himself from his biological farm which he had been taking care of for twenty years, several observers mention the possibility that the Queen decides, after her 95th birthday in 2021, to "pass the torch to Charles". However, they point out that this would not be an abdication of the Queen, but a period of regency in which Charles would be given greater powers by his mother.

Public image and personality

Since Elizabeth II has given only rare public interviews, little is known about her private views. As a constitutional monarch, she does not express her political views in public. She has a strong sense of religious and civic duty and takes her coronation oath very seriously. In addition to her official religious role as Supreme Governor of the Church of England, she attends both that church and the Church of Scotland. She has shown her support for interfaith dialogue and has met with the leaders of other churches and religions including four popes: John XXIII, John Paul II, Benedict XVI and Francis.

Elizabeth II is a patron of over 600 organizations. Her main interests include horseback riding and dogs, especially Welsh Corgis, which she has been passionate about since 1933, and Dookie, the first Corgi owned by her family.

In the 1950s, at the beginning of her reign, Elizabeth II was considered a "fairy tale queen". After the trauma of the war, the period of progress and modernization was presented as a "new Elizabethan era". Particularly unusual were Lord Altrincham's words in 1957, accusing her speeches of being those of a "smug schoolgirl". In the 1960s, the monarchy tried to project a more modern image by making the television documentary *Royal Family, which* showed the royal family in everyday life, and by broadcasting the investiture of Prince Charles. The Queen took to wearing brightly colored overcoats and ornate hats that allowed her to be easily seen in a crowd.

At her silver jubilee in 1977, the crowds were truly enthusiastic, but press revelations about the monarchy in the 1980s increased criticism of her. Elizabeth II's popularity continued to decline in the 1990s and under public pressure she was forced to pay an income tax and open Buckingham Palace. Disaffection with the monarchy peaked after Diana's death, although it diminished after the Queen's speech six days later.

In November 1999, Australian voters rejected the abolition of the Australian monarchy in a referendum. Polls in Britain in 2006 and 2007 showed strong support for Elizabeth II' and referendums in Tuvalu in 2008 and St. Vincent and the Grenadines in 2009 rejected Republican proposals.

Personal wealth and investments in tax havens

Elizabeth II's personal fortune has been the subject of much speculation over the years. *Forbes* magazine estimated in 2010 that her assets would be worth about $450 million, but an official statement from Buckingham Palace in 1993 called the £100 million estimate "grossly exaggerated. Jock Colville, who was one of his private secretaries and the director of his bank, Coutts, estimated his wealth in 1971 at £2 million (equivalent to about £23 million in 2012). The *Royal Collection* (which includes works of art and the British Crown Jewels) is not personally owned by the Queen and is managed by a trust as are the royal residences such as Buckingham Palace, Windsor Castle and the Duchy of Lancaster, an investment portfolio valued in 2011 at £383 million. *Sandringham House* and Balmoral Castle are personal properties of the Queen. The *Crown Estate* portfolio managing the assets of the British Crown was worth 7.3 billion pounds in 2011, but is independent of the queen.

In 2017, the *Paradise Papers* revealed that the Duchy of Lancaster, which manages the Queen's private funds, had invested 7.5 million pounds in 2005 in an investment fund based in the Cayman Islands, a tax haven. A small part of this amount was also invested in the household appliance chain *BrightHouse (en)*, which was accused by the British authorities of using aggressive sales methods, and ordered in October 2017 by the *Financial Conduct Authority* to repay 16.6 million euros to 249,000 customers; however, the finance director of the Duchy of Lancaster, Chris Adcock, says he was unaware of having invested in *BrightHouse.* In addition, £5 million of Elizabeth II's money was invested in the *Jubilee Absolute Return Fund*, a fund based in Bermuda and then Guernsey (both tax havens), which invested in speculative markets; the Crown denies that it received any tax benefits from this. The offshore investments revealed by the *Paradise Papers* were previously undisclosed, leading to criticism of the lack of transparency of investments made with Elizabeth II's private funds.

Ancestry

Descendants

Elizabeth II is the mother of four children (Charles, Anne, Andrew and Edward), grandmother of eight grandchildren (William, Harry, Peter, Zara, Beatrice, Eugenie, Louise and James), and great-grandmother of ten great-grandchildren (George, Charlotte, Louis, Archie, Savannah, Isla, Mia, Lena, Lucas and August).

Titles and honors

Full title

Elizabeth II holds numerous honorary military titles and ranks throughout the *Commonwealth*, is the sovereign of many orders in her realms, and has received honors and distinctions around the world. She officially holds a different title in each of her realms: *Queen of New Zealand* in New Zealand, *Queen of Tuvalu* in Tuvalu, etc. In the Channel Islands and the Isle of Man, which are dependencies of the Crown, she is referred to as Duke of Normandy and Lord of Man respectively. In some territories, her official title includes "Defender of the Faith" and "Duke of Lancaster".

It is known successively under the titles of :

- April 21, 1926 - December 11, 1936: *Her Royal Highness* Princess Elizabeth of York
- December 11, 1936 - November 20, 1947: *Her Royal Highness* Princess Elisabeth
- November 20, 1947 - February 6, 1952: *Her Royal Highness* Princess Elizabeth, Duchess of Edinburgh
- since February 6, 1952: *Her Majesty* the Queen

Weapons

From April 21, 1944 (her 18th birthday) until her coronation, Elizabeth II's coat of arms consisted of a lozenge bearing the Royal Arms of the United Kingdom differentiated by a label of three silver points; the central point bearing a Tudor rose and the other two, a cross of St. George. Upon her accession to the throne, she inherited the various coats of arms used by her father during his reign.

Enjoy all our books for free...

  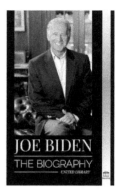

Interesting biographies, engaging introductions, and more.

Join the exclusive United Library reviewers club!

You will get a new book delivered in your inbox every Friday.

Join us today, go to: https://campsite.bio/unitedlibrary

BOOKS BY UNITED LIBRARY

Kamala Harris: The biography

Barack Obama: The biography

Joe Biden: The biography

Adolf Hitler: The biography

Albert Einstein: The biography

Aristotle: The biography

Donald Trump: The biography

Marcus Aurelius: The biography

Napoleon Bonaparte: The biography

Nikola Tesla: The biography

Pope Benedict: The biography

Pope Francis: The biography

Bitcoin: An introduction to the world's leading cryptocurrency

And more...

See all our published books here:
https://campsite.bio/unitedlibrary

ABOUT UNITED LIBRARY

United Library is a small group of enthusiastic writers. Our goal is always to publish books that make a difference, and we are most concerned with whether a book will still be alive in the future. United Library is an independent company, founded in 2010, and now publishing around up to 50 books a year.

Joseph Bryan - FOUNDER/MANAGING EDITOR

Amy Patel - ARCHIVIST AND PUBLISHING ASSISTANT

Mary Kim - OPERATIONS MANAGER

Mary Brown - EDITOR AND TRANSLATOR

Terry Owen – EDITOR